Home SWEET Home

Frances Lincoln
Children's Books

A home isn't a home without a pet!

That's what we think, anyway, but maybe we're biased!
We live right here, in the pages of this book—but if you
could live anywhere in the world, where would you choose?

A sleepy village in France, like our pal Bonaparte?
Or London, like Queenie, whose human walks her along
the River Thames every day? Or would you live in Brooklyn,
like the lucky cats who wake up to the New York skyline
every morning?

Peek inside apartments, houses and backyards as
our friends lead you on a journey around the world.
Where would you choose as your home sweet home?

My human, Jack—that's the man fishing over there—runs a guesthouse in Cape Cod. People say we're a lot alike. We've both got white hair and we growl when we're hungry. In the summer, our house is packed with people, and Jack's always saying, "Get out of the kitchen!", but the visitors love me. They feed me bacon and call me "Good boy", even though I'm actually an old man. In the winter, the house is quiet. Jack's granddaughter visits sometimes. She takes me for long walks along the beach, and feeds me popcorn as we watch TV. But I can't wait till spring when the house will be full of games and laughter again.

VINCENT—AMSTERDAM, THE NETHERLANDS

The best thing about Amsterdam is that people cycle everywhere. My human puts me in his basket and we ride through the city, peeking in at windows as we pass. Lots of the houses are tall and thin, but they're all different inside. Ours is the best—but I have to share it with a cat.

ARUN—KAY LAR YWA, MYANMAR

My name means "Sun", because I'm the light of everyone's life. Can you see me? I'm sitting next to my human, waiting patiently for him to catch more fish for me. I live in a wooden house that stands on stilts above a calm blue lake. People get around by rowing, and we cats sometimes hitch rides to see our friends—but mostly we just jump from roof to roof.

I'm Rex, king of the block. The houses around here each have their own personality, just like the people (and pets) that live in them. The only trouble is, the streets are so hilly that I get out of breath just chasing a ball!

This side of the street belongs to me and my sister—other cats don't dare come near. We roam the big gardens at night, hunting mice, but we don't stray far. A few blocks away are busy streets packed with people from all over the world.

DRAGO—CAPRI, ITALY In the summer, our tiny island is full of visitors, so I stay right here at home with my humans. They're excellent cooks—they make fresh pasta, risotto, or local fish, and they always save some for me.

ANIKA—GIETHOORN, THE NETHERLANDS

I know I don't look it, but I'm very old for a cat—almost twenty—so this peaceful village suits me. Cars aren't allowed here, so we walk or travel by boat. The only sound is the rustling of the trees, and sometimes the tweeting of the birds . . . though I'm too old to chase them!

CHANG—HONG KONG, CHINA

Oh, hi there—sorry if I look sleepy, I was just having a nap. I live in a tiny apartment, and the noise from the street is always waking me up. There's usually something interesting to eat, or sniff, or bark at around here. Like that kitten everyone is fussing over . . .

DULCE—IBIZA, SPAIN Life is peaceful in Ibiza. I laze around all day in our house, which is painted white to reflect the sun and keep us cool. In the evenings, when the sound of cicadas fills the air, I stroll outside to relax. But it isn't very relaxing when my humans start playing music . . .

I live in a village built beneath rocky cliffs, at the edge of the stormy sea. This place suits me—I'm as big and solid as the rocks that surround us, and my thick fur keeps out the cold. People don't have fur, though, so the roofs of the houses are covered in grass to keep them warm. The buildings look as though they're growing out of the Earth itself.

TAIKI—KYOTO, JAPAN

Kyoto is calm and full of ancient things—
like me. Tortoises can live to be a hundred!
The walls of my house are made of paper, and
there are no stairs, so I can crawl wherever I
like. Very slowly.

いえ

CHURRO—MEXICO CITY, MEXICO

Mexico City is like lots of little cities in one, and wherever you go you'll see dogs. I live on the top floor—that's me on the balcony—but I'm always visiting my friends in other apartments, like Chica the Chihuahua who lives downstairs.

QUEENIE—
LONDON,
ENGLAND,
UK

This is me, with my little human, Laura. She lets me sit on the couch when her parents aren't around . . . I walk her to school every day along the River Thames, where ancient churches stand next to brand-new skyscrapers. London is a city full of stories, waiting to be explored.

I'm a lucky cat—I wake up to the New York skyline every morning. I never get tired of the view. Manhattan is beautiful, whether the sun is shining or the snow is falling . . . and the snow often falls here in winter. After breakfast, my human lets me out of the apartment and I roam the city all day, taking in the sights and sounds and smells of New York. But I'm always pleased to see her when she gets home.

Paris is the city of love. We would know—we have a bird's eye view! The city is most beautiful at sunset, when the Eiffel Tower is silhouetted against the evening sky. We look out over the roofs as the sun goes down, watching the lights flick on all over the city, like stars.

JUAN—SEVILLE, SPAIN Our house is built around a courtyard, so it's always filled with light. The humans come home for a siesta in the hot afternoons. We relax together on the cool, tiled floors, until they go out again. Then I go back to sleep.